A Job for Raccoon Mike and Ralph Wolf

PAGE PUBLISHING
Conneaut Lake, PA

First originally published by Page Publishing 2023

ISBN 979-8-88960-351-1 (pbk)
ISBN 979-8-88960-368-9 (digital)

Printed in the United States of America

A Job for Raccoon Mike and Ralph Wolf

Patrick Hughes

"Hey, crew! I am Mike, and this is my friend,…

Ralph.

We are electricians on a construction site.

Today, we are wiring street-lamps on a playground.

Goals: How to work together as a team

We became friends at school. We met
at our special education class.

When they were in elementary school, Mike was easily distracted, which made school hard but not impossible.

Please Sit
Quietly

Ralph found it hard to sit still, so Ralph and Mike would help each other and became really good friends.

Trade
School

So when they got older and graduated school, the friends decided to go to trade school, and they became electricians.

I got it, I got it.
Where's my Flashlight?
13

Ralph gets "SUPER EXCITED" when they are starting a new job. Mike is always the boss at the construction site.

Some tools that they use are hard hats,
safety vests, goggles, work boots, tool belt,

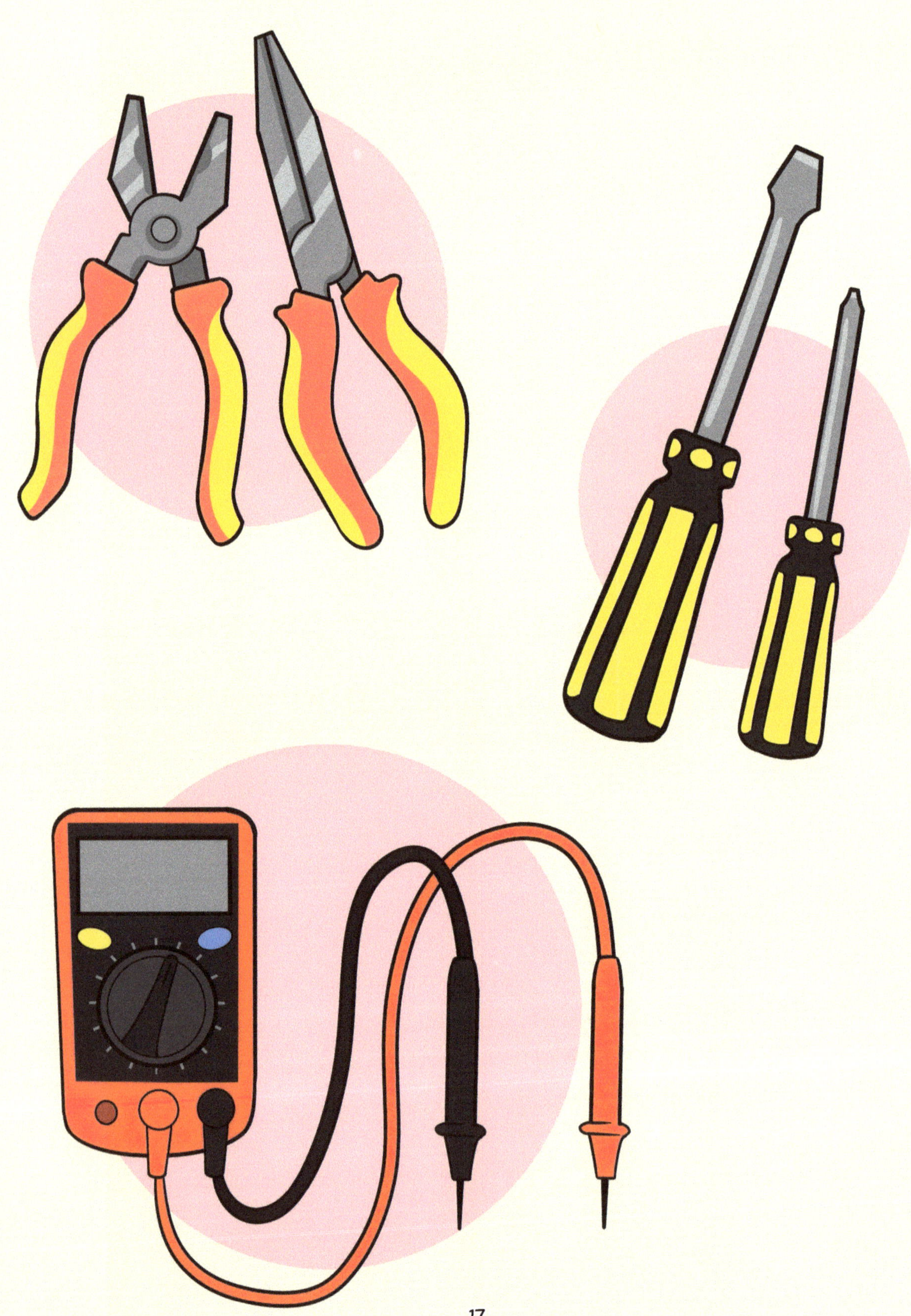

screwdriver, pliers, and voltage meter.

Electricians do the wiring so you are able to turn your lights on and off.

OFFICE
APARTMENT
BUILDING
SCHOOL
HOSPITAL

Electricians do the wiring for schools, hospitals, apartment buildings and houses.

At the end of a job, Mike looks over all the work that the crew and Ralph have done. Mike says, "Great work, crew. Wrap it up!"